Memories in Green

Memories in Green

BETO CONDE

MCM Books
January 2019

Copyright ©2019 by Beto Conde

All rights reserved. No part of this publication may be reproduced, stored in a retrieval system, or transmitted, in any form or by any means, without the prior written permission of the publisher, nor be otherwise circulated in any form of binding or cover other than that in which it is published and without a similar condition including this condition being imposed on the subsequent purchaser.

Published in the United States by MCM Books, Hutto, Texas.
All rights reserved.

ISBN: 978-0-9967473-4-9

Library of Congress Control Number: 2018962319

Dedication

Dedicated to mothers of every man, woman, and child murdered in wars.
May the impossible peace find your heart someday.

Introduction

I started writing about my experience in the Vietnam War as an escape, as my avenue of release for the tensions I felt inside. The thoughts and feelings etched in my mind, my heart, my soul needed a place to breathe. These thoughts and opinions on my journey from being drafted to PTSD are what this book is about. The relatively short time I spent in Vietnam has left me with a lifetime of nightmares, silent depression, emotional wounds, and paranoia called PTSD, that I have learned to live with over the years.

I grew up in South Texas and was drafted in 1967 along with many of my friends from the barrio I lived in. After four months undergoing Basic and Advanced Infantry Training in Fort Polk, Louisiana I was sent to Vietnam where I spent thirteen months before I was discharged as a Specialist Fourth Class. That was my entire military career, it lasted a total of nineteen months.

In November 2007, I was selected from nationwide entries to read my poem, "Mrs. Lake's Third Grade Class," at the Vietnam Memorial Wall in Washington, DC as a tribute on the Wall's 25th Anniversary celebration. The poem is dedicated to the memory of Timoteo "Tito" Santiago, Antonio "Tone" Hernandez, and Sigifredo "Güero" Montalvo Jr., for their ultimate sacrifice. The four of us were together from grade school through high school, and I wanted to honor them by reading the poem next to the Wall where their names are forever etched like their memory is etched in my mind. I have always felt some degree of guilt speaking publicly about my friends who did not return like I did, but I also feel an obligation to write about them to honor their memory.

In November 2007, on the occasion of the 25th Anniversary of the Vietnam Veterans Memorial Wall in DC, the author read a tribute to his classmates who died in Vietnam.

Ben Sherwood's book entitled *The Survivors Club, How to Survive*

Anything, served as an inspiration to write my book. Sherwood's book is about how people survive when the odds are impossible. I am also always reminded of a quote by the author Elie Wiesel who wrote, "Whoever survives a test, whatever it may be, must tell the story. That is his duty." This too inspired me to write about my experiences in the War.

One example is depicted in "War Mothers," where I tell of a close-up firefight, in which I made two decisions that I think are the reasons for my survival. When my squad was ordered to go bring back a wounded soldier from another squad, I made Decision Number 1. I exchanged my M-79 for an M-16 knowing the 79 would not be effective in the thick jungle we were in. When the enemy behind the green shadows sprang an ambush, some of my comrades panicked, even tried to run, but they were unable to do so through the thick jungle. Although I too feared we were all going to die, I made Decision Number 2; to follow my instincts, which told me that the only way to survive was by killing and not being killed. Sometimes situations do not give you a choice.

"War Mothers" is only one of several pieces in this book which convey thoughts of my mother and the mothers of all veterans. "El Cima y El Sima" ("The Height And The Depth") is the piece I have wanted to write since the day I returned from Vietnam. I wanted to share how exhilarating being involved in combat can be. How it feels to be alive at the height of one's existence and knowing your life can end any second, both feelings at the same time.

Another piece close to my heart is "My Friend Noel" in which I remember when we met and how I saw our "enemy" very early in my tour; I saw them as fellow human beings. I, along with many others, saw the futility of the war. I saw the futility of it and wanted no part of the killing and the dying. Nobel Prize winning author Ernest Hemingway once wrote, "War is a crime; ask the Infantry and ask the dead." This piece reflects my defiance and attitude towards war.

I wrote, "Agent Orange Blues" as lyrics to a song. It talks about how the effects of war will live inside you for the rest of your life, and there is no escaping it. You can leave the war behind as the long years go by, but the many years will never completely erase what the war has made you.

While I survived, the War never leaves me. When I returned doctors diagnosed me with post-traumatic stress disorder (PTSD). I always worry about the effects of Agent Orange. Of course, most of my fellow Vietnam veterans suffer these and other consequences of the war, but what are we to do? We were called to serve and that we did at great personal sacrifice.

These stories provide a glimpse into my experiences in Vietnam, which I hope others will relate to. After being involved in combat and surviving and witnessing others who did not, I have come to realize the futility of war. I'm reminded of the quote by John Steinbeck, "All war is a symptom of man's failure as a thinking animal."

My feelings are, as a species, by this time man should have evolved to where our primary goal in life on this planet is to provide a safe world for all its inhabitants, especially our children.

x - Memories in Green

Table of Contents

Dedication v
Introduction vii
Soldier Boy 1
Moonlight Faces 2
Barrio Noises 3
Brainwash Before Sunrise 4
The Color Green 7
Choppers 9
MIA 10
Niños 11
Mrs. Lake's Third Grade Class 12
The Boy I Knew 14
On The Edge of The Edge 15
Carnales 16
Fire Mission 17
El Cima Y El Sima 19
Soldier Me 21
Rage 25
Wounds 26
Day of the Dead 27
War Mothers 28
Agent Orange Blues 31
Body Parts 33
Elephant at the Airport 35
A Father's Promise 37

Soldier's Dream 38
Waking Up Dead 39
Coyote 40
Distant Fire 42
The Rain 45
My Friend Noel 48
Talking to The Moon 51
Puro Gravy 52
Demons 53

Soldier Boy

Fallen soldier
    your mother weeps
Fallen soldier
    little sister calls
Soldier Boy
    your friends remember
Soldier Boy
    they can't picture you in the heat of combat
Soldier Boy
    your smiling face always ready with a joke
Soldier Boy
    you wouldn't try to kill
Soldier Boy
    boy forever
Soldier Boy
    an empty space was left in every heart, you ever touched.
Boy Soldier
    for you time stands still

Moonlight Faces

First time away from home
In the darkened dawn, a young man stood
at attention, as well he should.

Rows and rows of boys around.
"Hear my words," a Captain said.
Moonlight showered faces heard,
"War is here," the Captain said.

To rows and rows of faces soft,
"Death is near," a Captain said.
To faces young filled with fear,
"This trip home may be your last,"
the Captain said.

To boyish stares of disbelief,
"To take a bride will not be best,
for death is a cruel wedding gift,"
the Captain said.

"They who cared for you since birth
should get the money that comes
with the wooden box," the Captain said.

"Let your mother's pain, and tears mourn
by coffin draped in stars and stripes
and not a young girl in widow's dress,"
the Captain said.

Long ago, one darkened dawn,
to terror filled moonlight faces,
I heard a Captain say.

Barrio Noises

When the barrio noises die down,
And you no longer hear
children playing, cars passing, dogs barking.

When darkness covers the sky above
and stars light up the night.
When the family has gone to sleep at last
and the house is finally quiet,
She kneels in a corner of her bedroom floor:

A corner showered with the soft glow of candlelight;
Pictures and statuettes of holy saints
and Jesus Christ adorn her little altar.
The little jar of holy water is almost empty.
A steady stream of words whispered through barely parted lips.

Every night, for a long time she quietly prays.
Pleadings for family welfare and salvation
are made with comforting faith.
Years ago, both sons away at war
peace of mind was nowhere found.

There was nothing to ease the pain
But for that special corner:
that corner with the dancing lights and shadows

Where faith in God gave her strength
and brought peace and love
that kept my mother sane.

When the barrio noises died…

Brainwash Before Sunrise

In the dark before dawn
With fifty new soldiers keeping time
Jungle boots pounding pavement
Left right left, left right left

strong bodies honed for weeks and weeks
Ten mile run piece o' cake
left, left, left

one voice heard in the dark
"Ain't no use in looking down?
Ain't no discharge on the ground"
Left right left, left right left, left, left, left

A hundred boots pounding down
Left, left, left
fresh minds broken down
Left, left, left
Double time marching to something new
Kill, kill, kill
A new moon looking down
fifty voices a single sound
Kill, kill, kill
A hundred boots concert in rhyme
Keeping time, keeping time
Left right left, left right left, left left left
fifty soldiers turning into one
One mind for one aim
Kill, kill, kill

In the dark before dawn
Fifty new soldiers keeping time
Jungle boots pounding pavement
Left right left, left right left

One soldier keeping time
Pounding in the thought
Kill, kill, kill

One sound before daybreak
A hundred boots pounding pavement
Left, left, left
Tic toc, tic toc, the time is coming
Kill, kill, kill

A hundred boots hitting pavement
Left, left, left
Fifty voices before sunrise
Kill, kill, kill,

Brainwash in high gear
In the dark my voice too
Kill, kill, kill

Goosebumps
Kill, kill, kill
the hair on the back of my neck
Kill, kill, kill

Time to kill is coming it will not stop
boys becoming killers
Tic toc, tic toc

into killers
War is waiting
Tic fucking toc
No stopping the clock

In the dark before dawn
Fifty soldiers keeping time
Jungle boots pounding pavement
Left right left, left right left

Brainwashing before sunrise
Not me, I didn't see, I wouldn't see

No matter a hundred times
Kill, kill, kill
Not me

Kill, kill, kill
A thousand times
Not me
Not my mind

Not me

The Color Green

My heart is pounding wildly against my chest. In the silence, I can hear myself breathing, and I hear pounding in my head. My eyes search the shadows and the dark green crevices of the thick jungle that surrounds me. I look all around for any sign that another human being also dressed in green is somewhere in the shadows waiting to put my life to a sudden end.

Today I'm the last one walking in a long line of boys dressed in green. Any moment the sudden crack of an AK-47 breaking the jungle silence could be the last sound I ever hear. The jungle is full of noises, quiet noises full of urgency.

We walk out onto a sunny clearing of beautiful green grass. It is a lovely spot of natural beauty but very deadly, making easy targets of all of us as we walk out in the open. Full of fear, I walk across this clearing toward a line of trees. With every step I take, my green jungle boots flatten out the tall green grass leaving a wet trail of morning dew behind. As I walk back into the dark jungle again, vines and thorns trip me and grab at me telling me I don't belong.

The constant fear of death grips my every thought. Like many others, I think of the possibility of just getting wounded and being sent home. Maybe I wouldn't die, only lose my legs or perhaps just my arms and legs. But what if a land-mine blows me to little pieces? What if there aren't any pieces of me left big enough to send home to bury? What will my mother think? How would she feel? What's my mother going to do?

With thoughts of various horrible possibilities rushing through my mind, I continue my intense search of the jungle around me. I open my mouth to breathe and hear better as I listen for any little noise that will give them away. I search to my right and my left carefully and fearfully, knowing that the jungle waits in silence, ready to spill terror and death upon us at any instant. Fear tightens its grip on me.

"Bring up the rear," they told me, "they like to sneak up behind us."

Every few minutes I stop and turn around. I squat down for a moment. I look back and study the green jungle we just walked through. I watch and listen for movement or any other indication that someone is following us. I look for some Asian boy dressed in green aiming his weapon at the back of my head, ready to pull the trigger, not knowing what a friendly, peaceful person I am.

I continue my daily trek in this dark green jungle, my insides screaming, "I don't want to be a part of this brutal insanity." But no sound comes from my mouth.

The sixty-pound pack on my back gets heavier with my every step. At times, I have to grab vines or anything else I can to pull myself up the steep jungle mountainsides.

In my hands, a high-tech killing machine capable of firing 13 pieces of murderous lead per second, ready to tear some mother's son's flesh and shatter his bones splattering bits of him on the jungle floor.

Son to be no more.
No doubt some peaceful, friendly, young man
who doesn't want to be here
in this jungle
wearing green.
Someone
just like me.

Choppers

Flying just above the treetops,
chopper blades spinning above my head,
I look down at the green, dark green, and darker green jungle below
 getting closer and closer.

I don't know what's down there this time,
but I know we have no choice,
they are going to drop us into the green hell below.

On the way out,
choppers come to pick us out of the bush
to take us to a fire-base or some other safe area
I felt like we had just found the door out of hell,
even if only for a while
and wait 'til the next fateful drop

MIA

On the rim of a black volcano
deep in the jungle mountains of South Vietnam,
I found them resting on their backs,
faces decayed to the bone.
I didn't think to look
how death had claimed their bodies.
In the recklessness of youth,
I rifled through their pockets
that I may find a souvenir.
Fellow soldiers had arranged their bodies:
They lay side by side.
All four fully clothed in military green.
Must have been a hasty retreat;
Out of respect though short on supplies
they didn't take their comrades clothes.
I didn't stop to think
of families left up north.
Mothers, wives, sons, and daughters
will never know where they lay for eternity,
forever Missing in Action.

Niños

Niños entre labores de algodón
A lado del Rió Grande
Inocente mente jugábamos de soldados
¡Qué momentos! "Que fanaso"!
No sabíamos del terror

La inocencia se acabo
En un país muy lejano
Como soldados otra vez
La guerra nos consumió
Y aquel juego termino

En otro lado de este mundo
oí aquel silbado de me barrio
Pensé que era una ilusión
voltee a ver, y tu sonrisa me saludo
Ese encuentro nuestro
En la amistad de violencia
Pretendí ser soldado
Escondí me cariño y emoción
Los cubrí con miedo y precaución
Perdona mi comportamiento
La guerra me cambio

Mi cuerpo no tiene heridas
Las llevo en el corazón
Amigos de niños, guardo tu recuerdo
El resto de mis días

En tu viaje eterno Timoteo
Que Dios te guarde en paz
Y no conozcas guerra
nunca jamás

Mrs. Lake's Third Grade Class

fading memories of childhood friends;
fading memories of distant lands-
many days and years have passed
since we stood side by side that day.
time together was too brief;
you were in pain.
I, in my Vietnam survival mentality-
you were afraid.
I was angry and defiant;
you were subdued.
my words were tough:
our words were too few.
my manner was hardened;
words were too quick.
How could I know?
the last to see you alive
I remember your smiling face
with only hints of our youthful times
your empty smiling face

I saw that day
will be in my thoughts forever more.
That war killed your mother, too, that day.
Tito, my childhood friend,
farewell
on your journey home,
farewell.
Today
your name is on a shiny wall of black
along with Antonio Hernández
and Fred Montalvo,
remember?
They were with us in
Mrs. Lake's third-grade class

The Boy I Knew

The timid sort in the second grade.
Uprooted from the first grade to a new school a hundred miles away.
Lost his nerve when his world was turned upside down.
No different than the others in "first," withdrew into a shell in "second."
Staying there for a long time.
Not aggressive, not even assertive, timid in the sometimes cruel
 playground games.
The kid from "first" inside waiting for the right time to come out,
He knew that time it would be for "keeps."
Holding back attracted aggression from tough little bullies the first
 couple of years.
By sixth grade, he was one of the boys.
In junior high, it was hard to blend in, especially on rainy days.
Muddy shoes announcing your side of town;
street paving there still on the back burner at city hall.
Many kids had clean shoes, even on rainy days.
It's harder to compete with clean shoes.
The Red Badge of Courage, called the boy, its meaning, questioning
 self.
 Always felt the courage would be there when the time came.
But when would that be?
Waiting, so long, created doubt of its existence and it faded and was
 finally forgotten.
The answer to the Red Badge of Courage came at last as a foot soldier.
They gave the medal for bravery to someone else with clean shoes.
He was the brave one, no medal needed, suffice the knowledge of a once
 timid boy.
That kid from first grade always knew he would emerge when it was for
 keeps.
Maybe not a hero, but overwhelming passion about staying alive.
And with those around me. That's what I did.

On The Edge of The Edge

I miss being on the world stage
In a war where the whole world is watching
I miss the adventure
I miss the risk
I miss going to the edge
I miss the overwhelming fear
I miss living on the edge
I miss the rush of surviving those frantic moments
I miss the brotherhood
I miss the wild excitement of partying on off-limits streets
Mocking the danger on the edge of the edge
I miss my youth
Where did it go
seconds, minutes, hours, days, weeks, months, the speeding years
Lost space and time,
Stolen before my very eyes
My very eyes
were witnesses unaware
until I looked back and saw
it was gone

Carnales

[This piece is not from my experiences but was told to me by a fellow soldier. It stayed with me through the years. I tell "Carnales" in the first person as it was told to me.]

In 1968, he was in Vietnam serving as the FO (Forward Observer) for an artillery unit attached to an infantry unit out in the bush.

"We were out on patrol when we made contact with a unit of North Vietnamese Regulars," he begins. "My job was to call in a fire mission. I got on the radio and called my unit."

'This is Bravo Company calling for an 8888, on longitude 678, latitude 876 over.
¿'Oye brodita, de donde eres tú'? the voice came back on the radio. It blew me away.
'Soy de Harlingen vato. ¿de donde eres tú'?
'Yo soy de Brownsville vato.'
'Parece que pegamos con chingos de NVAs.'
'Ahorita les damos en toda la madre carnal.'

"I didn't think my South Texas accent was that noticeable. I never talked to him again."

Over the years he always asked any Vietnam Vet from Brownsville that he met if he was the voice on the other end that day he called in the fire mission. After many years later he had not run into him.

Fire Mission

The boys are in from the Bush
Back in Base-camp
away from the killing, away from the dying
escaping to the Enlisted Men's Club,
the EM club, where every day is a Holiday
all the beer you want and a USO show up on the stage
live music from back in the world
The club is packed, Boys from different units all over Base-camp
In from the bush
wild-eyed boys guzzling beer
the place is wild
good rock music, loud rock music
Above the voices, above the music
"Fire Mission" a voice comes from one of the tables
heads turn "Fire Mission" more voices
Boys get up and walk out the door
hands reaching into oversize jungle fatigue pockets
Out the door around the side
Everyone knows, no need to hide
It's everywhere, grass and OJs
"Fire Mission"
kids from big cities back in the world
country kids
small town kids
together for the first time
Skin colors don't matter here
all painted green
Brothers who never met before
Looking for the great escape
"Fire Mission"
Fire up the weed, pass it down
Hand to hand, the mota goes 'round

A white boy talking shit, laughing
Black boys laughing
bonds from the bush
silent brotherhood deafening
"don't mean nothing"
J's and OJ's round and round they go
Coughing up smoke
Demons going up in smoke
"don't mean nothing"

Frantic firefights out in the jungle
Boys out in the bush
fire missions called in
artillery, mortars, gunships, fighter jets
death is in the air

fire mission outside the EM club
light 'em up, pass 'em around
friendly fire mission outside the EM Club
escape is in the air

getting high above it all
brothers from the bush
together for the first time
brothers from the bush
together for the last time

El Cima Y El Sima

I've never felt as alive as I did right after I almost died.
I stood at the summit of my very existence
In those frantic seconds of surreal calmness
I found myself face to face with death and
my life

Hace muchos años yo probé el sabor puro de lo que es realmente estar vivo.
En la mesa donde vida y muerte ambos se alimentan
pase unos acelerados momentos violentos
Ahí Aprendí como vivir el resto de mis anos

I've never felt as alive as when I almost died
I climbed up to a point where I realized how alive I really was
It was the same place where
I realized how easily one can die

Hace muchos años probé el sabor puro de lo que es estar vivo
En el hogar donde habitan los destinos
Parecía perder mi vida
Pero en defensa propia, yo mismo me rescaté

I've never felt as alive as when I almost died
I looked through the gates of hell down the other side into death and
    darkness
I got to the edge, stood there forever
turned around and walked away
more alive than ever before

Hace muchos años probé el sabor puro de lo que es realmente estar vivo
Momentos que no volveré a vivir jamás.
Segundos partidos en mil pedazos
Donde pasé toda una vida y Sobreviví

I've never felt as alive as when I almost died
when I realized I was still alive.
my heart still pumping
slow motion back to real-time
surreal back to real

I've never felt as alive as when I almost died
Those fleeting seconds I lived in slow motion long ago
always near me
Shattered seconds lasting lifetimes
forever etched in my mind

Ahora vivo mis años tranquilo,
No me falta nada
Pero
Hay momentos que me visita un lento pensamiento
Quisiera por un minuto nada más
Probar de nuevo esa violencia espantosa y
volver a sentir segundo por segundo lo que es verdaderamente estar vivo

Now and again a passing, fleeting thought finds me
The violence, the fear, the horror, the triumph calls me
Deep in the depths of my mind, lives a yearning to go there once again
To feel genuinely alive every single second that passes through me
I stood at the edge, the summit, where a black hole is one step away, one
    second away
but I didn't fall in

Yo permanecí
Pero un pedazo de mi corazón, mi alma, de mí
No, ahí quedó

Soldier Me

Some days in our lives stay in our minds as vivid memories that forever seem to have happened just yesterday. I'm going to share one of those days that I have carried with me for almost 40 years.

After a bout with malaria, I was on my way back out to the bush to join the rest of the guys from my company. They were operating in the remote jungles near the Cambodian border west of the town of Buôn Me Thuôt. We had our Transit Area on the outskirts of that town.

The "transit area," was a re-supply base located half-way between our Division Headquarters base camp, the rear, and the front lines, the bush. After landing there, I was walking to my Battalion area when I ran into a GI I knew from advanced infantry training back in the states, Roberto Maya from El Paso. He was one of the lucky ones who worked in the transit area. Maya invited me to go to downtown Buôn Ma Thuôt to check out the bars that night.

That afternoon Maya came by to pick me up, and we headed out walking to downtown Buôn Ma Thuôt. It was only a couple of miles from the US compound. Later on that night we wound up in a club located somewhere on the second story of some building. I didn't have any idea where we were. I was just following Maya around. I didn't know or care if the club was off limits. I was keenly aware that was death lurking all around. People were dying just a few miles outside the town. There were worse things that could happen to me than being thrown in the stockade for being in a bar.

The club was full of GIs. There were beautiful Vietnamese girls all over the place. There were a bunch of officers in the crowd too. I was somewhat resentful of all of them because these guys who worked in the rear, in the transit area had a chance to unwind and get away from the war in places like this. Not the guys in the front lines, the grunts, Boonie rats, ground dogs. Everything except for the jungle was off limits all the time for us, the Infantry. You could tell right away who the infantry guys were; they were dirty, grubby and too often wandering around with a blank stare in their eyes.

Maya hadn't told me he was planning on going home with one of the Vietnamese girls after they closed the bar. Just before they closed, he came over to me and said, "I'm going home with a girl, find yourself one so you can go home with her."

"I can't do that man. You have to take me back to transit; I don't know where the hell I'm at." I couldn't believe he was leaving me just like that. He just laughed and walked away.

I wasn't ready for that at all. I wasn't prepared to be in Chuck's (VC) backyard in the middle of the night without a weapon. I got highly excited on the inside. A little later, Maya brought one of the girls over and said I could go home with her. She smiled and took my hand. Then they started closing the club. Everyone left and disappeared into the night. I didn't have a choice, we stepped outside on to the street, and I followed the girl as she started walking to her place. I had no idea where I was. There were no lights anywhere, the whole town had shut down. We walked deeper and deeper into the back streets of a residential area. I knew this area was off limits to GIs for sure.

Being in combat or being close to its sudden possibility brings on a mentality of constant surveillance and diagnosing of every situation. After being in the bush around the clock non-stop for several months, I got used to the possibility of all hell breaking loose at any moment. I was always in what I now call my Vietnam survival mentality.

This was my first time alone with a Vietnamese girl. I was wired so tight, I paid very little attention to her. I kept looking around and behind us, as we walked in the dark with the moon and the stars were the only light. I was suspicious of every noise and every turn we took. Several times I grabbed her hand and pulled her with me with my back against the wall to look around and behind us. Each time she would smile and say "OK no problem, no problem here." I had been in the bush the whole time up to then and didn't know any other way to behave. I felt naked, exposed, and vulnerable without my M-16.

After walking down several streets, alleys and between houses, we finally got to her place at the end of a dark, narrow alley. It was a small room with a small stove, a table, two chairs, and a small bed. We had been there only for a little while when she asked me if I was hungry. I told her I was. In all the excitement, I hadn't eaten anything since that morning when I left Base Camp back in Pleiku.

She went out into the night saying she would be back in a little while with some hamburgers for us. As I waited, I started getting paranoid. As soon as she walked out the door, I regretted letting her go out and leaving me there alone and defenseless. Where was she going to find hamburgers in Vietnam at 3 o'clock in the morning? I didn't yet know you could get pretty much anything you wanted anytime for the right price. The black market in Nam was in full swing 24 hours a day.

She had been gone for about half an hour. As I waited, I got more and more paranoid. I was in the middle of a Vietnamese town in the middle of the night without a weapon. Everyone knew that night time was always Charlie's time, that's when they moved around and did the most damage. I got extremely nervous and began searching around in the little kitchen and found a knife. A few minutes later I heard someone walking outside in the alley. I hid behind the door as the girl came in. I waited there, silently, just in case she had brought company who was looking to do me in. She walked in and was surprised to find me gone. She turned and was startled when she saw me in the shadows behind the door with a knife in my hand. She realized the state of mind I was in and tried to calm me down. "No VC here, no VC here," she kept saying. I settled down somewhat, and we ate the burgers.

Afterward, we lay down on the bed, she was careful not to get me more suspicious than I already was, so we just laid there. I heard some noises outside in the alley, grabbed the knife and started to get up.

"No VC here, No VC here, you OK here," she repeated.

She chuckled and said it was only a dog. I didn't lie back down. I sat on the bed with my back leaning against the wall with the knife in my hand. She fell asleep next to me, every once in a while, she would wake up and tell me everything was OK. "You safe my house." I didn't sleep. My Vietnam survival mentality wouldn't let me. Sex was the last thing on my mind. First thing in the morning, I walked out and found a main street and hitched a ride back on a military truck.

What has kept this incident in my mind all these years is how the powers that be brought that young girl and me together that night. I never forget the chance meeting of two young people from entirely different worlds. We came together for completely different reasons and were heading in completely different directions in our lives. I would never see her again, and she would never see me again. I will wonder forever what became of her life. I will remember her forever and wish I had talked to her and told her how we were both mere pawns in the giant happenings around us called WAR. I wish I had taken some comfort in her arms away from the absurdity of the violence. Most of all, I wish I had told her we were not so different after all. She was trying to survive in the situation she was thrown into. I was trying to survive the situation I was thrown into.

When I reflect on that day, I am reminded of how the war changed me. I got inside myself and made survival my one and only focus. I think about that hardened soldier I became during that time and find it hard to believe I was him.

Rage

I never told
when I returned. I don't know why, but
I couldn't tell anyone.
I kept it inside,
raging, hurting.
They wouldn't understand:
brains spilled on the grass and weeds;
minds not coping, changing.
I couldn't explain that to anyone who wasn't there.
even I thought I wasn't there
pieces of hot steal zinging by my head-
it couldn't have been me.
It must be a dream.
How can anyone understand?
I was there and
I don't understand.
That's why
I never told.

Wounds

Not so long ago
My feet knew shoes only on special days
English was someone else's tongue
Mom was always home, my father was not
School was the door to another world
Not so long ago I was an American I know
'Til doubt was thrown in my face
My bare feet touched the life of mother earth
The stars were a gift from God
Life was simple and good
Not so long ago
There were boys
Not so long ago there was war
There was death
There were wounds
Too deep for healing to reach

Day of the Dead

One day of the dead I never forget
Was the day three soldiers were killed
Soon after I was first sent out to the bush
We were humping up a jungle mountain in three lines
Sometime around midday, we stopped for a much-needed rest
Three men teams were sent out to guard our flanks
After a few minutes, we heard the rapid fire of several weapons
No one will ever know how it happened
Maybe they were not as vigilant as they should have been
Maybe they hadn't realized death was forever lurking in the green
    shadows
Maybe the enemy's experience in war was just overwhelming
Surprise and kill the enemy, they were dreadfully good at it
Their bodies were brought back to the line wrapped in their ponchos
Lifeless boots dangling out of the ponchos
If I close my eyes, I can still see those boots
Maybe it was just their day to die
El Día de los Muertos
Maybe they were only three kids who didn't belong in war
Maybe no one belongs in war
In war, every day is, el Día de los Muertos
Today on this
The Day of the Dead
The boy from Mattapan, Maryland, the boy from Durham, North
    Carolina, the boy from Madison, Wisconsin.
May you be in a better place

War Mothers

From the fire-base, we went down to the bottom of the mountain into the jungle valley. We usually camped down on the high ground, but it got late on us, so we had to dig in at the foot of the mountain. Most times, we planned where we would dig in for the night, but this time we didn't have a choice. As customary, we sent out three or four teams to recon the surrounding area. The rest of us went about digging holes setting trip flares, unloading packs, chowing down, etc. We hadn't been there twenty minutes when we heard some small arms fired close by. This was right after we had seen the abandoned battalion size NVA camp a couple of miles before. So, I naturally thought the worst, here we are a 120 GIs being attacked by 1,500 NVA. Right after we heard the shots, one of the squads that went out on recon from our platoon ran back into the perimeter, minus one.

The story they told was that he was pulling point and spotted several NVA and when he turned around to warn the others he got hit in the neck and fell. His buddies got so shook they took off running and left him behind. When they got back to the company perimeter the Captain heard what happened he pulled out his 45 and put the gun to the squad leader's head and yelled for him to get the fuck back there and bring him back. He didn't know the squad leader had been wounded slightly. At this point we didn't realize how bad the guy left behind was hit. Their squad was so shaken that the Lieutenant decided to send our squad. I was carrying an M-79 which wasn't very effective up close in the thick jungle. We were in a really dense jungle down at the bottom of the valley. I gave my M-79 to a buddy and took his M-16.

I had never been so terrified in my life; everyone in the perimeter felt sorry for us but were glad they weren't the ones that had to out to get our man left behind.

We walked for about 50 yards crawling the last 15 until we came to a small clearing. A body was lying motionless in the center of the clearing. I thought it was a Vietnamese soldier at first. Not until I saw his glasses did I realize it was our man, he had bled out and changed colors. The guy was big, so the squad leader picked the two bigger men to go get his body, Alvarado and me.

We were all laying one behind the other on a trail about fifteen yards from the body. Alvarado was the closest to the body, and I moved up right behind him. Alvarado crawled up to the body and tied a belt to his wrist moved, back and pulled it. When he pulled the belt, and it came loose, it was getting dark, so Alvarado decided the hell with the booby traps and got real close to the body and started to raise it. Just then a burst of machine gun opened up, Alvarado fell to the ground yelling in Spanish. He was calling for his mother screaming in pain. By this time our squad leader, a black guy named Fox, had crawled up next to me at the head of the trail and started firing to where the fire came from. I started talking to Alvarado in Spanish for him to keep calm and crawl towards us. He started crawling, he was crawling on just his arms, dragging his legs that were shot up so bad he couldn't move them.

I saw an arm come out of the bushes and throw a grenade at us, I tried to sink my head into the ground and yelled "grenade." I got that from the movies because we were never taught that in training. That grenade got Alvarado in the legs and rolled him over several times. The screaming got louder, I talked to him some more trying to keep him from going into shock, telling him he was going to be alright, just a couple of feet more to go where I could grab him. Fox had started firing at them as soon as the shit broke out. They threw two more grenades at us that didn't explode. One landed not more than three feet from the machine gunner's face. The machine gunner just froze in shock waiting for the explosion to blow his head off, but the blast never came, it was a dud. They threw three grenades at us, and only one exploded, the one that got Alvarado in the legs.

He kept screaming, and I kept telling him that he was close enough where I could get to him. Fox kept firing about one or two inches above Alvarado's head to cover him. I stopped shooting, I was afraid he would raise his head and get hit by my fire. Our machine gunner opened up firing into the bushes where their fire came from. The gunner back at the perimeter opened up with is M-60 to confuse the enemy as to what direction our fire was coming at them. Finally, after what seemed like a long time Alvarado was close enough to us. I crawled up to him about two or three yards and raised him up and put him on my shoulders. Fox kept firing to cover us.

I carried him back close to the perimeter then the Lieutenant took him from me and carried him rest of the way. The backs of both his legs were a bloody mess. He screamed even louder when somebody accidentally touched his legs to help carry him.

By the time we got back to the perimeter, it was already dark. When we got back, the Lieutenant called in a Medivac. The jungle was too thick and tall for a landing. They dropped a sling and put Alvarado in it, and they flew away. We inherited his pack, the things he left behind, his C-rations, cigarettes, pillow. I got his lighter. The next morning one of our patrols found our body, flies crawling all over his face. They also found a dead NVA soldier, his buddies had taken his pants, they were hard up for supplies.

I've heard that the last words many who die in a war say is to call for their mother. I've never forgotten Alvarado's screams for his mother that day.

Mothers don't go to war, but they are with there with us. A soldier carries a weapon to defend himself, but mothers don't carry a weapon to protect their boys, all they have are their prayers.

Agent Orange Blues

I got the Agent Orange blues
Sprayed over my head and on my jungle bed.
Orange poison from hell sprayed 30 years ago
Are now closing in on me.
Lord, they just won't let me be.

I got the Agent Orange blues
come back to find me just like that!
Can't shake it loose and that's a fact;
It's the big one I'll have to pay-
Man, this devil just won't go away.

I got the Agent Orange blues
and Uncle Sam won't listen to what I have to say.
I said I got the Agent Orange blues
And Uncle Sam just wants to look away.

I got the Agent Orange blues;
Oh Lord, I think I'm dying,
And the government says I'm lying.
After they forced me to fight,
It just doesn't seem right.
I got the Agent Orange blues
And Grandma's yerbas just won't do.
I got me Agent Orange deep inside.
Oh Lord, I don't know where to hide.

Woke up this morning;
Nothing is where it should be:
up is now my down;
Lord, I'm headed for the ground.

I said
I got the Agent Orange blues,
But, man, the fact is
Agent Orange
now got me

Body Parts

Where are all the body parts?
Pieces of arms,
Sets of hands,
Legs,
Just one foot
Rib cage parts
And eyes,
Lost forever
In the jungles, the deserts, the forests, the mountains and valleys
Where are the wounded soldiers today?
They're everywhere
On the battlefield screaming
At home thinking suicide
In VA hospitals
In Nursing Homes for the young
Limping along through life
In the dark
Blind in one eye or blind in two
Pieces of face
Left behind with many dreams of a "normal" life
Fortunately, but unfortunately, the torso and the head are still alive
Some will go on with life
Some minds will not
Minds forever trapped
In the pain and horror of those split seconds when time stopped
Minds lost with the other body parts and left behind
Politicians who make unnecessary war,
Do not fight them
They and theirs are home safe
They get to keep their body parts
How can they not know?
About the young people's body parts

To be strewn on the sand
How can you not know?
About the body parts left behind
Scattered about or disappearing in a flash of fire
Lost in the sand
Lost with the ignorance to the horrors of war
Lost with the confusion about patriotism
Lost among the lies and the deception
Tomorrow will bring lucrative contracts for those who make war and
    profit from it
Tomorrow will not bring back the body parts,
Body parts left behind by those brave soldiers
They are lost forever.

Elephant at the Airport

You stand out among the jeans and bright colors everybody else is
    wearing.
You in your camouflaged fatigues of brown and sand.
Alone in the crowds of people coming and going

Soldier at the airport, where are you heading?
Is this your safe return to the world you left behind?
Back from hell, never to be the same again.
Or this a possible one-way trip to forever?

Soldier at the airport
On your journey of life or death
What is behind those eyes?
Is it the fear of the unknown that waits for you at the other end?
In your mind, a thousand thoughts racing I know
Will this departure from loved ones at the airport be the last goodbye?

Those eyes staring far beyond what you can see.
You're all alone in crowded terminals.
Walking in a daze, among a haze of people
People far removed from the other reality you will soon discover
People far removed from the explosions.
Not you, explosions wait patiently for soldiers like you
to drive by in a camouflage of sand and brown.

Life never stops going around in circles.
I've seen that look in your eyes, another time another life
Soldier at the airport
You're the elephant in the room,
a grim reminder noticed by few
while others pretend not to see

Will you die soldier in the crowd
To stay forever young
Or will you live to an old age like me
to witness young soldiers at the airport coming or going
and wonder?
And look at those eyes that hide everything on the inside
and wonder
When will it end

A Father's Promise

No words were ever spoken
on the day of my return.
Still in my uniform,
he took me to church.
We walked up to the altar-
We both knelt down in
silence.
A few minutes passed-
I guess he thanked God
for my safe return.
We got in the car;
drove home;
no words were ever spoken.

Soldier's Dream

Too old to be a soldier
again, dressed in military green.
How did I get here?
I know what to do; I know I can survive.
But, what if I don't?
I did the first time
When I was very young.
I know what to do.
I know I can survive.
In the mist of my fear
I must not panic.
I know what to do.
But, WHY me again?
I already served.
I got out alive.
Maybe I didn't.
Where am I?
My heart is pounding!
I can't breathe;
in fear and panic,
I wake up!

Waking Up Dead

I slowly regained consciousness
I didn't know where I was
I was laying down sleeping
As my mind was coming to awareness out of my seeming coma
I sensed someone was moving behind me as I lay on my side
I felt this overwhelming sensation that whoever was behind me
Was about to stab me, shoot me, kill me
I was paralyzed in my sleep coma
I tried to move but
I couldn't move to defend myself
I wanted to lash out with my right hand
To strike at the person or persons behind me
My limbs were not responding
I was paralyzed with sleep in dreamland trying to escape the fear that
    was real, the real dream
I struggled and struggled for what seemed like forever
Forcing my mind from a deep sleep to fully awake self-defense
I was paralyzed in my sleep coma
I couldn't move to defend myself
The dream was a dream
The fear was real
I couldn't figure out where I was
I knew I was in danger
I had to do something
I couldn't move at all
I was paralyzed, helpless
I was about to die
Just as I woke up
In the safety of my bed at home

Coyote

He stopped on the far side of the street and looked back.
Our eyes met for a shattered second.
I sensed a connection
I saw survival
In my mind, I saw his soul
in those wild yellow eyes flashing by,
I thought I saw, my soul,

A coyote dashed across the road in front of me.
Already at full speed, before he got to the road,
before he streaked across my eyes.
Running from something, someone before looking back,
vision collision, connection
our eyes met, his panicked, mine amazed.

Coyote your eyes on fire,
surviving the overwhelming odds
Surviving among not so kind humankind
I saw the panic, the courage, the strength in eyes flashing at my eyes.
Forever on the alert, always ready to run for your life, literally.

I sensed the panic, the courage, in your eyes flashing at mine.
And stopped in my tracks to admire you,
I wanted to relate my respect and admiration.
Impossible but to my mind
I wanted to share, I recognized where you are.
The fear, the courage, the strength to survive the odds

I salute you Coyote on the run
I admire you Coyote on hyper vigilance
Once I was you
Sometimes I am you
Flashing across my eyes
In the occasionally monotonous routine every day of our lives,
some days, something wakes you up again

I saw the Coyote say, I'm alive,
I Heard the Coyote say, you're still alive!

¡Un coyote con sus ojos del sol me dijo
estás vivo!

Distant Fire

[This piece also is not from my experiences but was told to me by a fellow soldier. I repeat it here as best as I remember it.]

El Pollo Caliente fried chicken stand wasn't what you would call a thriving enterprise. After the bills were paid, just enough money was left to keep things going. The word profit never did quite apply to amounts that meager, but sometimes that's they all they needed, just enough to keep going.

In the early morning hours, the small mom and pop fried chicken stand stood alone in silence. In the glare of a full moon, it cast the only shadow in the middle of the half block parking lot on Main Street. At that hour, the single movement in the six-block downtown area came from a couple of cars quietly slipping through the night.

Earlier, just before closing time at *El Pollo Caliente*, someone walking out pushed the double pan deep fryer back against the wall. Whoever had moved it forward to sweep behind it, forgot to push it back. The three-eighths inch copper gas line that was hooked up to it had been bent one too many times—it cracked; a tiny crack, unseen behind the fryer. The gas line began leaking a small stream of invisible gas inside the little stand. It took the small cloud of gas about four hours, first floating to the ceiling before it grew big enough to reach the pilot light on the little gas stove where they cooked the *frijoles*. Sometime around two-thirty in the morning it came.

BOOM!

The explosion was heard for blocks in all directions, ending an otherwise quiet night's sleep for many citizens of the little town.

Somewhere in another world, my friend was on his back fast asleep. Except for a few days here and there, he had been in the mountain jungles twenty-four hours a day for the previous eleven months. He remembered vividly every single day in all those months that he had been away from the jungle. The four days on a stand-down back in base camp was a blur of beer and pot. There were the seven days on sick call for jungle rot on his ankles. He almost talked the Army into sending him to a hospital in Japan on that one. Another time there was ten days in the hospital in Nha Trang for malaria—he missed getting killed with others from his unit that time. The last time was the five days in Hawaii on R&R, where the plan was to escape to México, but that hit a snag. That was it! The rest of the time he had been in the jungle with his squad every day and every night. His ears never completely shut down anymore, even when he slept.

Suddenly, he heard the eighty-one mortar round explode nearby. Experience told him it was about 50 yards from their position. No panic. That could get you killed. He casually rolled over to a prone position on the ground. Without any hesitation, he began low crawling to the foxhole bunker on the perimeter line a few feet away. He crawled up to the sandbags stacked three high on each side of the hole. Slowly, he raised his head just far enough where he could look over the sandbags. Staring at a fire, trying to figure out what was coming down, his hands groped around in the dark where he always kept his M-16. He stared at the fire for a full minute.

A little building on fire—something wasn't right. He'd seen this place before; it looked all too familiar. His mind raced, confused, staring, trying to make sense of it. Then, slowly, realization crept in. It was the chicken stand half a block down the street from his parents' house back in "the world." How could that be? Was he hallucinating? Was his mind playing games?

Then, out of nowhere, a smile appeared on his face. For a fraction of a second, the smile froze; he looked around at the walls of his bedroom to make sure. The smile came back. He slid down from the windowsill where he had been resting his chin.

He was home!

The sensation from the smile spread down to the rest of his body, shaking it with laughter as he rolled around on the floor in silence. He had one hand on his stomach and the other over his mouth to keep from laughing out loud. He didn't want to spook his parents again, for the night before while he was sleeping, he had stood up on the bed and pointed at the ceiling fan, yelling, "It's the chopper, it's the chopper." His own yelling woke him up. A bunch of emotions ran through him in seconds: fear, courage, confusion, embarrassment, joy, and finally, wonderment.

He was sitting on the bed when both his parents who had been sleeping in the bedroom across the hall, rushed into his bedroom to see what was happening.

"I was having a dream," he chuckled, trying not to worry them. "It's OK, it's OK." They looked at him with puzzled faces, and without saying anything, they went back to their bedroom.

This night, the shadows and lights from the distant fire came in through the windows into his bedroom. They danced on the walls around him, joining him in his quiet celebration.

He was home!

The Rain

Woke up to a silent sunrise alarm
My air mattress is comfortable despite the rough ground
After seven months living in the jungle
I'm used to our routine
Wake up, pack up, saddle up, gulp down cold C-rations
wait for the call to move out
Forming three lines, we head out into the dense jungle
Heading out to where only officers know and why
Our job is to be as vigilant as possible, as quiet as possible
We all keep our ever-present fear of "contact" inside and in check
The point man for the day is horrified as every second crawls by, way too slowly for him
He is out 25 yards ahead of the rest of us
all alone
He's the canary in our mine
and in our mind
If we do make "contact," he's 99 percent dead
With sixty pounds of essentials on our back
We hump through the silent jungle praying for no contact
Weeks without contact wearing on our nerves day after day
hour after hour fearing the nearly inevitable
hour after hour the odds getting worse
one afternoon as we continue our daily trudge it starts to rain
the word from the old timers is that the Monsoon has started

It rains every day for several hours
No choice, we get used to it
It's a light rain that goes almost unnoticed under steel helmets
but after an hour the moister finally penetrates fatigues on my shoulders
uncomfortable, but manageable
my rucksack keeps my back dry
eventually, the rain penetrates my fatigues
arms and legs now getting wet
uncomfortable, almost unmanageable
Soon after, my fatigues are completely soaked except down between my weary legs
The only comfort left
nearly completely soaked we hump in the rain for hours
wet misery second only to the always present fear
Finally, I feel my crotch getting wet and wetter
I remember feeling awfully sorry for myself. Finding myself there not of my choice. I just want to scream "fuck this shit," but I don't
I was a foot soldier
One late evening 40 years later
I walk out to the lime tree in my backyard,
To my surprise, a gentle rain has found me
I don't notice at first, but when I reach the lime tree
I remember the Asian rain from long ago
A Monsoon hello

As I reach up to grab a lime, the light rain falls on my hand
As the wet drops touch my bare skin
A flashback touches my mind!
I've been caught by the rain many times after Vietnam,
but the rain,
The rain had never talked to me before
I hear the rain say, "remember me?"
I do, you almost made me cry, I say to myself
As the wet drops touch my bare skin
Again, I almost feel like I almost want to cry.
But I don't,
Gentile monsoon raindrops
You sneaked up on me after all these years
Once I wanted to scream
I didn't
I'm alright now, I tell myself
I slowly deliberately scan the darkness all around me
I search for the ghost that's been haunting me
all these years
then
I turn around with one lime in my hand
and walk back to the present

My Friend Noel

After being in the jungles of Vietnam 24/7 for too many months
Somehow, we both wound up in Base Camp
We became the best of friends
A black kid from the ghetto streets of Brooklyn and
A Tex-Mex kid from the barrio streets of South Texas
We were a perfect match

After the being in bush for way too long
We got crazy, we were wild motherfuckers
Still in the Army but not soldiers anymore, in any way
We lost all respect for military authority,
We didn't care about anything anymore

When you walked into a room the lights came on
When you walked into a room smiles broke out
When you walked into a room everybody relaxed
You were a Cool Breeze during those hot days in Vietnam
That was your nickname in Nam My Friend
Everybody called you Cool Breeze

After two months of staying with a girl in downtown Pleiku
You, my brother Breeze
learned a Vietnamese song
Then you surprised and thrilled the girls we partied with
Singing their song

We lived, we ate, we partied, we got high, we got lost
we were together 24/7 living only for the moment
We were running partners living on the edge
We were partying in "off limits" areas in a war zone
We were in the enemy's back yard getting high with their women
We were risking everything like there was no tomorrow

No one knew your real name Noel, my friend
I heard it one time from an office clerk and never forgot it
Thinking Cool Breeze was a long way from Noel
When I was back in the world, you sent me two joints in a letter from Nam
Cool fucker, you made me smile all the way from the other side of the world

My friend Noel
35 years later I looked you up in the phone book in Brooklyn and found you.
Your voice hadn't changed, you answered "who's this?" Sounding exactly like you
I said, "it's Conde man"
You said "Condi, motheer fuck!"

After that
We got together one time in New York
Thirty-five years changed nothing between us
Brothers forever
We planned to get together again
We never did, we re-connected on the phone

As grandfathers, we laughed about the wild times
We talked about all the crazy things we did,
We talked about the great times we had,
We talked about how nothing else mattered
The times we went "off limits" to downtown Pleiku
Soul Music, beautiful Asian Women, and Opium Soaked Joints

We got busted for being off limits
The MPs found us asleep hiding on a rooftop downtown
We didn't give a shit, what were they going to do, send us to Vietnam?
"It don't mean nothing" was the answer to everything anyway

We remembered introducing the new guys coming in-country to OJ's
We told them it was so good we guaranteed to put a smile on their face
And it did and when they smiled
We broke out laughing
You and me, fuck the man's war!

I hadn't cried for anyone since Vietnam like I cried the day I got the
    phone call that you were DEAD!
Now that you have died, I feel a part of me died too
The wild, reckless kid you knew so well no longer exists
That Mexican kid who was just as fucking crazy as you were, died when
    you died

Hermano mio
I will miss you my friend,
We were running partners going 200 hundred miles an hour
Ignoring the danger, the risk
we outran the man and his war
It was the most exciting good times I will ever have
We were wild motherfuckers on a wild ride, in a wild place

I never knew how much I loved you until you fucking died
Noel, my brother
Cool Breeze, you AWOL motherfucker
my friend Breeze
Fuck you for not telling me you were dying.
And….
Fuck you for dying without telling me.

Talking to The Moon

I walked out into the night
A giant moon trying to imitate the sun
Moonlight falling everywhere lighting up the everything
Silver light casting shadows all about
A soft breeze swaying trees, moving shadows all about
Under a loud glow sprayed down by a bold moon face
one shadow walks with me, talks to me, calls me
Silver moon from the sky so far above talking to me
here we are again
Tell me how long has it been?
Lighting dark streets for me, mean streets I knew as a kid
Illuminating a young lover's face on lonely country roads
Lighting up millions of bright points of silver and gold on never-ending
    skies
those dark jungle nights you hid when I was becoming a man
You were watching us
Dime Luna, tell me where we're going, my old friend
Tell me about the shadow at my feet
Luna vieja so far away
close enough to touch me
Talk to me
Luna
Tell my shadow the story,
about me

Puro Gravy

Sitting here in the safety and comfort of my home,
a memory came and revealed itself.
I just remembered something I said a long time ago
surrounded by fear, greenery, loud noises, and death
in the middle of a war.
I said to myself,
"If I ever get out of here alive,
every day of my life will be gravy."
I was sitting here in my home
without a weapon in my hands.
No one is trying to kill me;
I don't have to kill anyone
and
I just remembered
every day of my life
es PURO GRAVY!

Demons

The shadows of Past Trouble Shit Days still haunt Carlos Martinez and the boys after all this time. We cross paths standing under the canopy outside the VA psych clinic. It's raining like hell, hard and steady without any sign of letting up.

We stand around and start telling old war stories while we wait for the rain to subside. Just another typical, friendly, "I know how it was," "I was there too," conversation with a fellow Viet vet with PTSD. Two familiar strangers, we laugh at the serendipity and the crazy similarities of those times long ago when we lived far apart in the same place.

We should be driving home alone by now, but no. The steady rain gets stronger and stretches our conversation longer where we cross an invisible line, and reveal secrets, suppressed emotions, and invisible wounds. We throw in some more macho laughter into the conversation to ward off lurking demons.

Suddenly, lightning!

With a flash of light that turns the day to a brighter white, the drenching sky injects itself into our fragile conversation. The deafening boom cracks the air around us and seriously startles me. Carlos Martinez's body jerks forward, his hands touch the sidewalk cement. He takes several steps sideways and turns around to face the rain.

"Fuck, that scared the shit out of me!"

He looks at me with a, you know what I mean look on his other face.

"That was damn loud man!" I look back at him still a bit shaken.

Carlos Martinez stands back up and regains his composure. He tries to talk but is unable to continue our conversation after the explosion of sound and light. A minute passes and like our conversation the rain slows down too.

He suddenly takes off running into the rain.

"I got to go man. Take care," he yells back over his shoulder.

He just takes off and leaves me there standing all alone needing some more Carlos Martinez conversation therapy.

Across the parking lot as he reaches out to grab the door handle of his truck, I see the demon that's been chasing him for 40 years about to catch Carlos Martinez and I close my eyes.

"Yeah, you too man," I yell back as I start running to my truck.

Running as fast as my old legs let me; I'm too scared to look back over my shoulder.

56 - Memories in Green

www.ingramcontent.com/pod-product-compliance
Lightning Source LLC
Chambersburg PA
CBHW060427010526
44118CB00017B/2393